ISBN-13: 978-0-9789678-4-0

WorkMatters
P.O. Box 130756
Birmingham, AL 35213 USA

205-879-8494
gayle@workmatters.com
WorkMatters.com

I DEDICATE THE WORKMATTERS LEADERSHIP JOURNAL TO MY CLIENTS,

whose commitment to their own goals inspired me to create this journal.

I am grateful for their trust in me, and for the opportunity to be a part of their leadership journey as they achieve what's most important to them.

Thank you!

"What you think about comes about. By recording your dreams and goals on paper, you set in motion the process of becoming the person you most want to be."
~ **Mark Victor Hansen**

About Gayle Lantz

Gayle Lantz is a leadership expert and founder of **WorkMatters, Inc.**, (www.WorkMatters.com) a consulting firm dedicated to helping leaders think and work smarter.

A sought-after consultant, executive coach, facilitator, and speaker, Gayle works closely with executives and leadership teams to expand their vision, think and act strategically, and inspire change. Together, they increase business results and help make work matter at every level of the organization. Among her clients are NASA, Microsoft, MassMutual, Southern Company, Lockheed Martin, BBVA Compass Bank as well as a variety of small and mid-sized professional service firms.

 Gayle runs senior executive roundtable groups comprised of executives from non-competing industries. Participants meet regularly to exchange ideas, sharpen executive leadership skills and gain objective perspective to help them grow their business.

Gayle is author of the award-winning book *Take the Bull by the Horns: The Busy Leader's Action Guide to Growing Your Business...and Yourself.*

Before starting her own business, Gayle worked as an executive in the insurance, financial services and investment industry. She most recently held an officer level position with TIAA-CREF -- a leader in its industry serving those in the academic, medical, cultural and research fields.

Gayle's articles and/or quotes have been featured in a variety of national and global business publications including *BusinessWeek, Harvard Management Update, Wall Street Journal Online, FastCompany.com, CEO Online* and *The New York Times.*

Gayle is a graduate of Emory University in Atlanta, Georgia. She lives in Birmingham, Alabama, and has been honored as one of Birmingham's Top 10 Women in Business.

CONTACT:
205-879-8494
gayle@workmatters.com
workmatters.com

Introduction

Studies show that you are much more likely to achieve your goals just by writing them down. Most people don't.

This journal is designed to help you accomplish what's most important to you this year. It's simple. And requires just a little discipline.

You can use it to help you take needed steps on a weekly basis to achieve what you really want in your leadership role, business and/or personal life.

A few reasons to write down your goals:

You will…

1. Gain needed clarity about what's most important to you and where you want to go.

2. Sharpen your focus. When you're highly focused on what you want to accomplish, you'll be less likely to be pulled in other directions.

3. Build momentum. It's motivating to see progress—step by step.

4. Increase your accountability. It's one thing to say you want to accomplish something. When you write it down, you will be more committed.

5. Increase your sense of accomplishment. No more being busy. You'll work with greater purpose and conviction—and get more done.

6. Accelerate your progress. With a clear target, you can move forward more quickly and strategically.

7. Communicate your goals more clearly to others. When you have a consistent way to express what you're trying to accomplish, other people can better follow or support you.

8. Be more decisive. You will have a better basis for decision-making.

9. Become more disciplined by focusing on what really matters to you on a regular basis.

10. Be able to look back and celebrate success!

So let's get started!

I'll ask you a few coaching questions along the way.
You'll also find quotes to keep you inspired.

Plan to spend 10-15 minutes each week to focus on what's most important to you.
If you get stuck or miss a week, simply get back on track. Habits take time to establish. Don't feel guilty or abandon the process. Jump back in and keep moving.

This is *your* process.
There are no grades. No judgment.
Just an opportunity to get clear and achieve what you *really* want.

Here are some questions to kick-start the process…

What's something you would be very excited to accomplish this year? In your work or in your life? Something that *you* really want? (Not what anyone else thinks you should want, what *you* really want.)

Be specific. What does it look like, feel like? Describe the scene in detail.

Why is the goal important to you?

What will it do for you or others?

How will you know you're making progress during the year? Any milestones or measures of success?

Make it BIG!

Believable. Is it something you really believe you can do?

I believe I can achieve this goal because_____.

Impactful. Is it something that will make a significant difference or impact?

The impact when I achieve this goal will be _____.

Gutsy. Does it make you a little nervous?

To overcome any nervousness or anxiety as I work toward my goal, I will

_____.

"At the moment of commitment, the entire universe
conspires to assist you."
~ Johann Wolfgang von Goethe

My BIG goal for the year is:

_____

_____

_____

_____

_____

_____

Once you're clear, determine what you will do each week to achieve your goal.

You may want to map out specific steps in advance to the extent you can. Or you can take one week at a time and figure it out as you go.

No pressure. Just focus.

A FEW TIPS TO GET THE MOST OUT OF YOUR
JOURNALING EXPERIENCE

TIP #1:

Be consistent. Spend time with your journal at the same time each week. Commit just 10 to 15 minutes. Put the commitment on your calendar

TIP #2:

Respond to each of the five prompting statements each week. They are all important. Don't overthink. Just write.

TIP #3:

Commit to specific timeframes or deadlines to see better results.
What will you do by when? Be as specific as possible when you commit to action.

TIP #4:

Use the "Notes" section to capture whatever bubbles up as you're thinking. Consider recording your action items there. It might be an unrelated idea, a concern, a hope, an image. There's no "right way" to use the space. Use it as you wish.

TIP #5:

Talk about your goals and ideas with a friend, coach, mentor, accountability partner—someone you trust in your network or mastermind group. You'll be even more likely to achieve what you want.

****

I wish you much success as you accomplish what's most important to you this year.

Let this leadership journal be one way to provide the assistance you need.
And let me know if I can be of any help along the way.

Your work matters.

Gayle

A Couple of Additional WorkMatters Resources

1. For additional insight to help you achieve what's most important, subscribe to my blog. Consider the blog a companion resource.

You'll find weekly motivation based on the quotes included in this journal.

Follow along each week to get a dose of timely inspiration as you accomplish your goals!

Visit: www.workmatters.com/blog

2. If you'd like a little coaching each day, download my free mobile app:

My Daily Coach

You'll receive a simple coaching message each day designed to keep you thinking and working smarter.

It's available for your smart phone or Ipad through the App Store or Google Play.

9

Week 1

Date: _____

"People with goals succeed because they know where they are going."
~ Earl Nightingale

My most important goal for this week is:

_____

_____

What I've accomplished since last week:

_____

_____

An opportunity I have or can create this week is:

_____

_____

What I've learned within the last week:

_____

_____

What I'm grateful for now:

_____

_____

NOTES

_____

_____

_____

_____

_____

_____

_____

_____

_____

_____

_____

_____

_____

_____

_____

Week 2

"You need to overcome the tug of people against you as you reach for high goals."
~ George S. Patton

My most important goal for this week is:

_____

_____

What I've accomplished since last week:

_____

_____

An opportunity I have or can create this week is:

_____

_____

What I've learned within the last week:

_____

_____

What I'm grateful for now:

_____

_____

NOTES

_____

_____

_____

_____

_____

_____

_____

_____

_____

_____

_____

_____

_____

_____

_____

Week 3

Are you paralyzed with fear? That's a good sign. Fear is good. Like self-doubt, fear is an indicator. Fear tells us what we have to do. Remember one rule of thumb: the more scared we are of a work or calling, the more sure we can be that we have to do it.
~Steven Pressfield

My most important goal for this week is:

_____

_____

What I've accomplished since last week:

_____

_____

An opportunity I have or can create this week is:

_____

_____

What I've learned within the last week:

_____

_____

What I'm grateful for now:

_____

_____

NOTES

Week 4

Date: _____

"Writing in a journal reminds you of your goals and of your learning in life.
It offers a place where you can hold a deliberate, thoughtful
conversation with yourself."
~ Robin S. Sharma

My most important goal for this week is:

_____

_____

What I've accomplished since last week:

_____

_____

An opportunity I have or can create this week is:

_____

_____

What I've learned within the last week:

_____

_____

What I'm grateful for now:

_____

_____

NOTES

Week 5

"When we are no longer able to change a situation - we are challenged to change ourselves."
~ Victor E. Frankl

My most important goal for this week is:

_____

_____

What I've accomplished since last week:

_____

_____

An opportunity I have or can create this week is:

_____

_____

What I've learned within the last week:

_____

_____

What I'm grateful for now:

_____

_____

NOTES

_____

_____

_____

_____

_____

_____

_____

_____

_____

_____

_____

_____

_____

Week 6

*"I don't focus on what I'm up against. I focus on my goals
and I try to ignore the rest."*
~ **Venus Williams**

My most important goal for this week is:

_____

_____

What I've accomplished since last week:

_____

_____

An opportunity I have or can create this week is:

_____

_____

What I've learned within the last week:

_____

_____

What I'm grateful for now:

_____

_____

NOTES

_____

_____

_____

_____

_____

_____

_____

_____

_____

_____

_____

_____

_____

_____

_____

Week 7

"What you get by achieving your goals is not as important as what you become by achieving your goals."
~ Zig Ziglar

My most important goal for this week is:

_____

_____

What I've accomplished since last week:

_____

_____

An opportunity I have or can create this week is:

_____

_____

What I've learned within the last week:

_____

_____

What I'm grateful for now:

_____

_____

NOTES

_____

_____

_____

_____

_____

_____

_____

_____

_____

_____

_____

_____

Week 8

Date: _____

"Keep your fears to yourself, but share your courage with others."
~ Robert Louis Stevenson

My most important goal for this week is:

_____

_____

What I've accomplished since last week:

_____

_____

An opportunity I have or can create this week is:

_____

_____

What I've learned within the last week:

_____

_____

What I'm grateful for now:

_____

_____

24

NOTES

_____

_____

_____

_____

_____

_____

_____

_____

_____

_____

_____

_____

_____

_____

Week 9

"If you want to build a ship, don't drum up the men to gather wood, divide the work, and give orders. Instead, teach them to yearn for the vast and endless sea."
~ Antoine de Saint-Exupery

My most important goal for this week is:

_____

_____

What I've accomplished since last week:

_____

_____

An opportunity I have or can create this week is:

_____

_____

What I've learned within the last week:

_____

_____

What I'm grateful for now:

_____

_____

NOTES

_____

_____

_____

_____

_____

_____

_____

_____

_____

_____

_____

_____

_____

_____

Week 10

*"If what you are doing is not moving you towards your goals,
then it's moving you away from your goals."*
~ Brian Tracy

My most important goal for this week is:

_____

_____

What I've accomplished since last week:

_____

_____

An opportunity I have or can create this week is:

_____

_____

What I've learned within the last week:

_____

_____

What I'm grateful for now:

_____

_____

NOTES

_____

_____

_____

_____

_____

_____

_____

_____

_____

_____

_____

_____

_____

_____

_____

Week 11

"Whenever you see a successful business, someone once made a courageous decision."
~ Peter F. Drucker

My most important goal for this week is:

_____

_____

What I've accomplished since last week:

_____

_____

An opportunity I have or can create this week is:

_____

_____

What I've learned within the last week:

_____

_____

What I'm grateful for now:

_____

_____

NOTES

_____

_____

_____

_____

_____

_____

_____

_____

_____

_____

_____

_____

_____

_____

Week 12

"We move in the direction of what we most frequently and deliberately ask questions about."
~ David Cooperrider

My most important goal for this week is:

_____

_____

What I've accomplished since last week:

_____

_____

An opportunity I have or can create this week is:

_____

_____

What I've learned within the last week:

_____

_____

What I'm grateful for now:

_____

_____

NOTES

Week 13

Date: _____

"Success is not final. Failure is not fatal. It is the courage to continue that counts."
~ **Winston Churchill**

My most important goal for this week is:

_____

_____

What I've accomplished since last week:

_____

_____

An opportunity I have or can create this week is:

_____

_____

What I've learned within the last week:

_____

_____

What I'm grateful for now:

_____

_____

NOTES

_____

_____

_____

_____

_____

_____

_____

_____

_____

_____

_____

_____

_____

_____

Week 14

"God gave me such a good brain that in one minute I can worry more than others do in a year."
~ Sholem Aleichem

My most important goal for this week is:

_____

_____

What I've accomplished since last week:

_____

_____

An opportunity I have or can create this week is:

_____

_____

What I've learned within the last week:

_____

_____

What I'm grateful for now:

_____

_____

NOTES

Week 15

Date: _____

"Life is like riding a bicycle. To keep your balance,
you must keep moving."
~ Albert Einstein

My most important goal for this week is:

_____

_____

What I've accomplished since last week:

_____

_____

An opportunity I have or can create this week is:

_____

_____

What I've learned within the last week:

_____

_____

What I'm grateful for now:

_____

_____

NOTES

Week 16

"It is not because things are difficult that we do not dare;
it is because we do not dare that they are difficult."
~ Seneca

My most important goal for this week is:

_____

_____

What I've accomplished since last week:

_____

_____

An opportunity I have or can create this week is:

_____

_____

What I've learned within the last week:

_____

_____

What I'm grateful for now:

_____

_____

NOTES

Week 17

"The great pleasure in life is doing what people say you cannot do."
~ Walter Bagehot

My most important goal for this week is:

_____

_____

What I've accomplished since last week:

_____

_____

An opportunity I have or can create this week is:

_____

_____

What I've learned within the last week:

_____

_____

What I'm grateful for now:

_____

_____

NOTES

_____

_____

_____

_____

_____

_____

_____

_____

_____

_____

_____

_____

_____

_____

_____

Week 18

"We cannot direct the wind, but we can adjust the sails."
~ **German Proverb**

My most important goal for this week is:

_____

_____

What I've accomplished since last week:

_____

_____

An opportunity I have or can create this week is:

_____

_____

What I've learned within the last week:

_____

_____

What I'm grateful for now:

_____

_____

NOTES

Week 19

"The pursuit of perfection often impedes improvement."
~ George F. Will

My most important goal for this week is:

_____

_____

What I've accomplished since last week:

_____

_____

An opportunity I have or can create this week is:

_____

_____

What I've learned within the last week:

_____

_____

What I'm grateful for now:

_____

_____

NOTES

_____

_____

_____

_____

_____

_____

_____

_____

_____

_____

_____

_____

_____

_____

_____

_____

Week 20

Date: _____

"Real change begins with the simple act of people talking about what they care about most."
~ Margaret J. Wheatley

My most important goal for this week is:

_____

_____

What I've accomplished since last week:

_____

_____

An opportunity I have or can create this week is:

_____

_____

What I've learned within the last week:

_____

_____

What I'm grateful for now:

_____

_____

NOTES

Week 21

"A good leader is a person who takes a little more than his share of the blame and a little less than his share of the credit."
~ John Maxwell

My most important goal for this week is:

_____

_____

What I've accomplished since last week:

_____

_____

An opportunity I have or can create this week is:

_____

_____

What I've learned within the last week:

_____

_____

What I'm grateful for now:

_____

_____

NOTES

Week 22

Date: _____

"Do your own thinking independently. Be the chess player, not the chess piece."
~ Ralph Charell

My most important goal for this week is:

_____

_____

What I've accomplished since last week:

_____

_____

An opportunity I have or can create this week is:

_____

_____

What I've learned within the last week:

_____

_____

What I'm grateful for now:

_____

_____

NOTES

_____

_____

_____

_____

_____

_____

_____

_____

_____

_____

_____

_____

_____

Week 23

"I believe that human beings are desperate, always, to belong to something greater than themselves."
~ David Whyte

My most important goal for this week is:

_____

_____

What I've accomplished since last week:

_____

_____

An opportunity I have or can create this week is:

_____

_____

What I've learned within the last week:

_____

_____

What I'm grateful for now:

_____

_____

NOTES

_____

_____

_____

_____

_____

_____

_____

_____

_____

_____

_____

_____

_____

Week 24

Date: _____

"Choosing our own aims and seeking to bring them to fruition creates a sense of vitality and motivation in life. The only things that derail our efforts are fear and oppression."
~ Brendon Burchard

My most important goal for this week is:

_____

_____

What I've accomplished since last week:

_____

_____

An opportunity I have or can create this week is:

_____

_____

What I've learned within the last week:

_____

_____

What I'm grateful for now:

_____

_____

NOTES

Week 25

Date: _____

"The most courageous act is still to think for yourself. Aloud."
~ Coco Chanel

My most important goal for this week is:

_____

_____

What I've accomplished since last week:

_____

_____

An opportunity I have or can create this week is:

_____

_____

What I've learned within the last week:

_____

_____

What I'm grateful for now:

_____

_____

NOTES

_____

_____

_____

_____

_____

_____

_____

_____

_____

_____

_____

_____

_____

Week 26

"Before you are a leader, success is all about growing yourself. When you become a leader, success is all about growing others."
~ Jack Welch

My most important goal for this week is:

_____

_____

What I've accomplished since last week:

_____

_____

An opportunity I have or can create this week is:

_____

_____

What I've learned within the last week:

_____

_____

What I'm grateful for now:

_____

_____

NOTES

_____

_____

_____

_____

_____

_____

_____

_____

_____

_____

_____

_____

_____

_____

_____

_____

Week 27

"The key to successful leadership today is influence, not authority."
~ Kenneth Blanchard

My most important goal for this week is:

_____

_____

What I've accomplished since last week:

_____

_____

An opportunity I have or can create this week is:

_____

_____

What I've learned within the last week:

_____

_____

What I'm grateful for now:

_____

_____

NOTES

Week 28

Date: _____

"Vision without execution is delusion."
~ Thomas Edison

My most important goal for this week is:

_____

_____

What I've accomplished since last week:

_____

_____

An opportunity I have or can create this week is:

_____

_____

What I've learned within the last week:

_____

_____

What I'm grateful for now:

_____

_____

NOTES

Week 29

Date: _____

*"The only thing that has to be finished by next Tuesday
is next Monday."*
~ Jennifer Yane

My most important goal for this week is:

_____

_____

What I've accomplished since last week:

_____

_____

An opportunity I have or can create this week is:

_____

_____

What I've learned within the last week:

_____

_____

What I'm grateful for now:

_____

_____

66

NOTES

Week 30

"Obstacles are those frightful things you see when you take your eye off the goal."
~ Henry Ford

My most important goal for this week is:

_____

_____

What I've accomplished since last week:

_____

_____

An opportunity I have or can create this week is:

_____

_____

What I've learned within the last week:

_____

_____

What I'm grateful for now:

_____

_____

NOTES

_____

_____

_____

_____

_____

_____

_____

_____

_____

_____

_____

_____

_____

_____

Week 31

"To think too long about doing a thing often becomes its undoing."
~ Eva Young

My most important goal for this week is:

_____

_____

What I've accomplished since last week:

_____

_____

An opportunity I have or can create this week is:

_____

_____

What I've learned within the last week:

_____

_____

What I'm grateful for now:

_____

_____

NOTES

_____

_____

_____

_____

_____

_____

_____

_____

_____

_____

_____

_____

_____

_____

Week 32

Date: _____

"There are no shortcuts to any place worth going."
~ **Beverly Sills**

My most important goal for this week is:

_____

_____

What I've accomplished since last week:

_____

_____

An opportunity I have or can create this week is:

_____

_____

What I've learned within the last week:

_____

_____

What I'm grateful for now:

_____

_____

NOTES

Week 33

"You must have long-range goals to keep you from being frustrated by short-range failures."
~ Charles C. Noble

My most important goal for this week is:

_____

_____

What I've accomplished since last week:

_____

_____

An opportunity I have or can create this week is:

_____

_____

What I've learned within the last week:

_____

_____

What I'm grateful for now:

_____

_____

NOTES

_____

_____

_____

_____

_____

_____

_____

_____

_____

_____

_____

_____

_____

_____

Week 34

Date: _____

"The greatest dreams are always unrealistic."
~ Will Smith

My most important goal for this week is:

_____

_____

What I've accomplished since last week:

_____

_____

An opportunity I have or can create this week is:

_____

_____

What I've learned within the last week:

_____

_____

What I'm grateful for now:

_____

_____

76

NOTES

_____

_____

_____

_____

_____

_____

_____

_____

_____

_____

_____

_____

_____

_____

_____

Week 35

"If you are going through hell, keep going."
~ **Winston Churchill**

My most important goal for this week is:

_____

_____

What I've accomplished since last week:

_____

_____

An opportunity I have or can create this week is:

_____

_____

What I've learned within the last week:

_____

_____

What I'm grateful for now:

_____

_____

NOTES

_____

_____

_____

_____

_____

_____

_____

_____

_____

_____

_____

_____

_____

Week 36

"It always seems impossible until it's done."
~ Nelson Mandela

My most important goal for this week is:

_____

_____

What I've accomplished since last week:

_____

_____

An opportunity I have or can create this week is:

_____

_____

What I've learned within the last week:

_____

_____

What I'm grateful for now:

_____

_____

NOTES

Week 37

"Real courage is when you know you're licked before you begin, but you begin anyway and see it through no matter what."

~ Harper Lee

My most important goal for this week is:

_____

_____

What I've accomplished since last week:

_____

_____

An opportunity I have or can create this week is:

_____

_____

What I've learned within the last week:

_____

_____

What I'm grateful for now:

_____

_____

NOTES

Week 38

"Don't dwell on what went wrong. Instead, focus on what to do next. Spend your energies on moving forward toward finding the answer."
~ Denis Waitley

My most important goal for this week is:

_____

_____

What I've accomplished since last week:

_____

_____

An opportunity I have or can create this week is:

_____

_____

What I've learned within the last week:

_____

_____

What I'm grateful for now:

_____

_____

NOTES

_____

_____

_____

_____

_____

_____

_____

_____

_____

_____

_____

_____

_____

_____

_____

Week 39

"Gratitude is the healthiest of all human emotions. The more you express gratitude for what you have, the more likely you will have even more to express gratitude for."
~ Zig Ziglar

My most important goal for this week is:

_____

_____

What I've accomplished since last week:

_____

_____

An opportunity I have or can create this week is:

_____

_____

What I've learned within the last week:

_____

_____

What I'm grateful for now:

_____

_____

NOTES

Week 40

"Perseverance is failing 19 times and succeeding the 20th."
~ Julie Andrews

My most important goal for this week is:

_____

_____

What I've accomplished since last week:

_____

_____

An opportunity I have or can create this week is:

_____

_____

What I've learned within the last week:

_____

_____

What I'm grateful for now:

_____

_____

NOTES

_____

_____

_____

_____

_____

_____

_____

_____

_____

_____

_____

_____

_____

_____

_____

_____

Week 41

"Patience is not simply the ability to wait - it's how we behave while we're waiting."

~ Joyce Meyer

My most important goal for this week is:

_____

_____

What I've accomplished since last week:

_____

_____

An opportunity I have or can create this week is:

_____

_____

What I've learned within the last week:

_____

_____

What I'm grateful for now:

_____

_____

NOTES

_____

_____

_____

_____

_____

_____

_____

_____

_____

_____

_____

_____

_____

_____

Week 42

Date: _____

"The more that you read, the more things you will know. The more that you learn, the more places you'll go."

~ Dr. Seuss

My most important goal for this week is:

_____

_____

What I've accomplished since last week:

_____

_____

An opportunity I have or can create this week is:

_____

_____

What I've learned within the last week:

_____

_____

What I'm grateful for now:

_____

_____

NOTES

Week 43

Date: _____

"If you really want to do something, you'll find a way.
If you don't, you'll find an excuse."
~ Jim Rohn

My most important goal for this week is:

_____

_____

What I've accomplished since last week:

_____

_____

An opportunity I have or can create this week is:

_____

_____

What I've learned within the last week:

_____

_____

What I'm grateful for now:

_____

_____

NOTES

_____

_____

_____

_____

_____

_____

_____

_____

_____

_____

_____

_____

_____

_____

Week 44

"The question isn't who is going to let me; it's who is going to stop me."
~ Ayn Rand

My most important goal for this week is:

_____

_____

What I've accomplished since last week:

_____

_____

An opportunity I have or can create this week is:

_____

_____

What I've learned within the last week:

_____

_____

What I'm grateful for now:

_____

_____

NOTES

_____

_____

_____

_____

_____

_____

_____

_____

_____

_____

_____

_____

_____

_____

Week 45

"To be yourself in a world that is constantly trying to make you something else is the greatest accomplishment."
~ Ralph Waldo Emerson

My most important goal for this week is:

_____

_____

What I've accomplished since last week:

_____

_____

An opportunity I have or can create this week is:

_____

_____

What I've learned within the last week:

_____

_____

What I'm grateful for now:

_____

_____

NOTES

Week 46

"Forget about trying to compete with someone else. Create your own pathway. Create your own new vision."
~ Herbie Hancock

My most important goal for this week is:

_____

_____

What I've accomplished since last week:

_____

_____

An opportunity I have or can create this week is:

_____

_____

What I've learned within the last week:

_____

_____

What I'm grateful for now:

_____

_____

NOTES

_____

_____

_____

_____

_____

_____

_____

_____

_____

_____

_____

_____

_____

_____

Week 47

"I have always argued that change becomes stressful and overwhelming only when you've lost any sense of the constancy of your life. You need firm ground to stand on. From there, you can deal with that change."
~ Richard N. Bolles

My most important goal for this week is:

_____

_____

What I've accomplished since last week:

_____

_____

An opportunity I have or can create this week is:

_____

_____

What I've learned within the last week:

_____

_____

What I'm grateful for now:

_____

_____

NOTES

_____

_____

_____

_____

_____

_____

_____

_____

_____

_____

_____

_____

_____

_____

Week 48

Date: _____

"Simplicity is the final achievement. After one has played a vast quantity of notes and more notes, it is simplicity that emerges as the crowning reward of art."
~ Frederic Chopin

My most important goal for this week is:

_____

_____

What I've accomplished since last week:

_____

_____

An opportunity I have or can create this week is:

_____

_____

What I've learned within the last week:

_____

_____

What I'm grateful for now:

_____

_____

NOTES

Week 49

"Never mistake activity for achievement."
~ John Wooden

My most important goal for this week is:

_____

_____

What I've accomplished since last week:

_____

_____

An opportunity I have or can create this week is:

_____

_____

What I've learned within the last week:

_____

_____

What I'm grateful for now:

_____

_____

106

NOTES

_____

_____

_____

_____

_____

_____

_____

_____

_____

_____

_____

_____

_____

Week 50

Date: _____

"The direction of your focus is the direction your life will move. Let yourself move toward what is good, valuable, strong and true."
~ Ralph Marston

My most important goal for this week is:

_____

_____

What I've accomplished since last week:

_____

_____

An opportunity I have or can create this week is:

_____

_____

What I've learned within the last week:

_____

_____

What I'm grateful for now:

_____

_____

NOTES

_____

_____

_____

_____

_____

_____

_____

_____

_____

_____

_____

_____

_____

_____

_____

Week 51

Date: _____

"Life's most persistent and urgent question is, 'What are you doing for others?'"
~ Martin Luther King, Jr.

My most important goal for this week is:

_____

_____

What I've accomplished since last week:

_____

_____

An opportunity I have or can create this week is:

_____

_____

What I've learned within the last week:

_____

_____

What I'm grateful for now:

_____

_____

110

NOTES

_____

_____

_____

_____

_____

_____

_____

_____

_____

_____

_____

_____

_____

_____

Week 52

"True happiness... is not attained through self-gratification,
but through fidelity to a worthy purpose."
~ Helen Keller

My most important goal for this week is:

_____

_____

What I've accomplished since last week:

_____

_____

An opportunity I have or can create this week is:

_____

_____

What I've learned within the last week:

_____

_____

What I'm grateful for now:

_____

_____

NOTES

_____

_____

_____

_____

_____

_____

_____

_____

_____

_____

_____

_____

_____

_____

CONGRATULATIONS!

You made it through the year!

I hope you've accomplished what's most important to you.
I'm sure there have been some highs and lows along the way. That's part of the process.

Trust that wherever you are now is exactly where you need to be and that things will unfold as they need to.

As you look ahead to another year, keep your focus on what you really want and visualize what the next level looks like to you.

Continue to move toward people or resources that offer support and inspiration. Move away from toxic people or negative influences that hold you back. You have much to look forward to and you can create it as you go.

I'd love to hear what you accomplished and hope you'll let me know if I can be of help as you conquer what's ahead.

Wishing you all the best in your leadership role, business and life.

Your work matters.

Gayle

CONTACT:

Also connect with me on LinkedIn:

Gayle Lantz
205.879.8494
gayle@workmatters.com
workmatters.com
WorkMatters, Inc.
PO Box 130756
Birmingham, AL 35213

https://www.linkedin.com/in/gaylelantz

Other Works, Resources & Programs
By Gayle Lantz

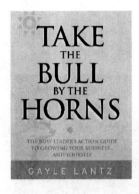

Available on Kindle

Available at
Amazon.com

For professionals who
want to take charge of
their career.

A comprehensive resource
for consultants, coaches or
other entrepreneurial types
interested in starting or
running mastermind
groups.

Special Online Program
for Women Leaders

All Available at
WorkMatters.com

Inspire change.
Your work matters.

GAYLE LANTZ
FOUNDER, WORKMATTERS, INC.

Book Gayle to Speak at Your Next Event!

Gayle speaks to groups, organizations and associations.

To book Gayle for an event, contact WorkMatters:
205.879.8494
admin@workmatters.com

NATIONAL SPEAKERS ASSOCIATION

CPSIA information can be obtained
at www.ICGtesting.com
Printed in the USA
LVOW09s1445201216
518106LV00003B/225/P